Annecy Tra (France

Discover the most up-to-date and amazing places to explore in Annecy, along with current information and guides on when to go, what to do, and the best places to see.

Hudson Miles

Table Of Contents

This travel guide provides helpful information. The ideas in the Day trips, Excursions, leisure activities, Itineraries in the city, and Neighboring cities are suggestions. You can craft and explore your vacation in your own style and preparation.

The attractions are listed with their opening hours, starting from the popular ones to the less-known ones. The map in this book provides some knowledge of the city, but the maps on your phone are more detailed. Consider taking screenshots as you walk around with no connection needed. Alternatively, you can contact the tourist office using the addresses and numbers provided in this guide.

If you have more time, explore both popular and less-known attractions mentioned in the notes below. Additionally, if you're interested in shopping, reach out to the stores or reach them through the contact numbers in this book.

For first timers, visiting or contacting the Tourist office, helps you get familiar with the city and it's attractions.

Lastly, try the travel prompts; they help enrich your travel experience and open avenues for personal growth.

The humor in the table of contents is included for an enjoyable reading experience.

Safe Trip....

The Haute-Savoie region's capital, Annecy, is a city of art with stunning architectural harmony. The historic town of Annecy is a genuine pleasure to explore. With its picturesque canals, flower-covered banks, modest quaint bridges, and gorgeous homes with vibrant facades, Annecy maintains its moniker of Savoyard Venice quite well. It's very wonderful to wander along its canals or explore the charming, winding pedestrian lanes.

The Annecy History museum is located in the Île palace, a former jail and the Palais de Justice (courts), in the centre of the old town. The Sainte-Claire street, which is nearby this iconic structure from the 12th century, is a must-see location because of its lovely arched dwellings. The museum-castle, which towers over the city and was once home to the dukes of Genevois-Nemours and the counts of Geneva, is devoted to archaeology, ethnology, art, history, and alpine lakes.

Nothing beats a stroll along the stunning Annecy lake's edge to cap off this lovely stay. Not to be overlooked! The Champ de Mars, the Albigny avenue lined with plane trees, the Europe Gardens, the Amours Bridge over the Vassé Canal, and all of these lovely locations are wonderful places to unwind. Visitors can rent pedalos and small motor boats or take a journey aboard tourist boats for the finest way to see the lake and nearby mountains.

There are many names for Annecy, including Venice of the Alps and Pearl of the French Alps. The city is the capital of Haute Savoie and is renowned for its lake and the grandeur of its landscape. The city is at the point of entry of the lake's cluse, surrounded by the opulent massifs of Bauges and Bornes. Plains and wooded hills, coniferous swaths, and a lake surrounded by extraordinary environment alternately make up the panorama. The metropolis primarily spans the plains in this breathtaking setting.

The second-largest natural lake in France and the first lake in Europe for water quality, Lake Annecy is perched at a height of 446 metres.

Important Gallo-Roman city Annecy earned the nickname "the Rome of the Alps" thanks to its prominent role in the Catholic Reformation. On March 24, 1860, during France's annexation of Savoy, it became the home of the Counts of Geneva and is unmistakably French. Annecy is a special place because of its compelling narrative, robust culture, and excellent natural setting. You have access to a wide range of recreational options.

ANNECY-THE-OLD: With more than 20,000 residents, Annecy-le-Vieux ranks as the fourth-largest city in the Haute-Savoie department. Its 1,700 hectares include 300 hectares of shared woodland, 1.7 km of Lake Annecy shoreline, 11.7 kilometres of the Fier River's bank, and 25 kilometres of bike routes.

CRAN-GEVRIER: Cran-Gevrier is a town in the Haute-Savoie region. It is situated on a hill in the midst of the Alps, a neighbourhood of Annecy. It has a remarkable natural environment with Chavanod or Poisy and both of those cities.

Because of its growth in the economy and tourism, the area is well renowned for being dynamic and imaginative. The area has been inhabited since Roman times, and a villa formerly stood there. Today, Cran-Gevrier is a popular tourist destination for people interested in exploring the Savoyard city's rich history. It also has a cultural influence because of its proximity to Annecy. The year-round availability of numerous cultural activities is another factor in Cran-Gevrier's success.

PRINGY: A charming city with a mountain climate, Pringy is a former little town north of Annecy. It is situated on the historic Geneva road, between Argonay and Annecy-le-Vieux, in the centre of Haute-Savoie.
Pringy, which is pleasant, is close to Lake Annecy, which offers the area a wonderful atmosphere and a little tempered climate. It received two flowers in the French contest for towns and villages for its lovely scenery and green areas. Close to the Swiss border, the town is great for visiting the remainder of the region or a very close neighbor.
The city of Pringy offers the chance to view an interesting architectural history built on old stones

and monuments in the manner typical of this region of the Savoy, in addition to outdoor activities and sports.

SEYNOD: Seynod, a town near Annecy known for the purity of its lake, sits at the intersection of major thoroughfares leading to Paris, Switzerland, Italy, and Germany. Seynod extends more than 10 kilometres to the west at the base of the Semnoz mountain, to the south-west of the Annecy urban area.
The 1965 and 1973 mergers with Vieugy and Balmont helped Seynod expand its territory and population. On July 1st, 1997, this merger became a full merger. There are approximately 18,000 people living in Seynod.
Seynod has become a complete city with urban and industrial infrastructure as a result. Today, the economic activity zones are home to close to 1,000 firms. The town of Seynod places a high premium on maintaining a healthy economy. The Périaz district, which has a total size of roughly 24 hectares and is situated in the southwest, partially along Provincial Road 1201, will enable the construction of new homes, businesses, and employment opportunities.

Seynod now has a true city centre with a bustling population. It is made up of the Hotel de Ville and Saint-Jean Squares, which are connected by the Paseo de Malgrat de Mar. Numerous stores and services keep these two squares and the Avenue de Champ Fleuri lively. proximity.

On the Place de l'Hôtel de Ville, the administrative centre officially debuts. Thus, it is very convenient to access the Town Hall, the Media Library, the Polyhedron, and the Auditorium.

Lake Annecy's tourism office may be found at CENTRE BONLIEU, Lac d, 1 Rue Jean Jaurès, 74000 Annecy, France. Its phone number is +33 4 50 45 00 33.

Day trips and Excursions

Below are suggestions on day trips and excursions, Embark on any of them to make your travel more enjoyable.

- Private Annecy and Geneva Sightseeing Tour (Historical Tours)
  - Time: over six hours

Explore Annecy, the "Venice of the Alps," which is renowned for its serene landscapes. The journey begins in rural France.

- Cost: $691 for each adult

- Wine Tour with Private Chauffeur
- Type: Spring Break - Duration: 6+ hours - Description: Travel comfortably and safely through the Combe de Savoie vineyards.
- Cost: $709 for each adult

- Guided Day Trip to Chamonix and Mont Blanc from Geneva

Take a panoramic glass-topped bus journey to take in the breathtaking Alps views. - Type: Cable Car Tours - Duration: 8-11 hours. includes a ride on a cable car.
- Cost: $178 for each adult

- Independent Chamonix trip with the Aiguille du Midi or the Mer de Glace

Tours using cable cars

Visit Chamonix and take in the renowned Mont Blanc on a guided trip. - Length: 8–10 hours. - Cost: $95 for each adult

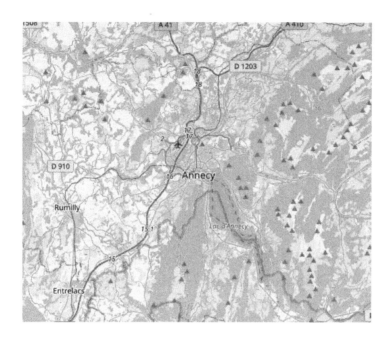

Plan and Pack

Research and Itinerary: Begin by learning about the fascinating history, popular tourist destinations, and delectable cuisine of Annecy. Make a flexible itinerary that covers famous sites like the Jardins de l'Europe (lakeside park) and the Musée-Château d'Annecy. Don't forget to stroll around Vieux Lille's lovely streets.

The best time to visit Annecy is in the late spring (April to June) or early autumn (September to October) when the city is at its most beautiful. The pleasant weather and less busy city make for a more immersive experience.

Accommodations: Whether it's a chic boutique hotel in the city centre or a charming bed and breakfast in Annecy, pick lodgings that suit your travel preferences. You'll get the best deals if you make a reservation in advance.

Annecy is a paradise for foodies. Try regional specialties like the renowned waffles and carbonnade flamande (beef stew). Discover the city's rich culinary culture, which includes both classic brasseries and modern bistros.

Be prepared for a range of weather conditions. For touring the cobblestone streets, you must have comfortable walking shoes, and even in the heat, you should bring a light jacket. For your electronics, remember to include a universal converter and a portable charger.

While English is widely spoken in the area, learning a few fundamental French words will improve your trip and win you the favour of the welcoming residents.

Your trip to Annecy, France, is going to be filled with fascinating experiences and a rich tapestry of cultural immersion. Our painstakingly produced travel guide has you covered whether you're exploring the colourful markets or indulging in delectable French cuisine.

Chapter 2

Basic french phrases and area slang terms to know before travelling.

- Bonjour (Hello)
- Merci (Thank you)
- Excusez-moi (Excuse me)
- S'il vous plaît (Please)
- Oui (Yes)
- Non (No)
- Comment ça va ? (How are you?)
- Parlez-vous anglais ? (Do you speak English?)
- Pouvez-vous m'aider ? (Can you help me?)
- Où est... ? (Where is...?)
- Combien ça coûte ? (How much does it cost?)
- L'addition, s'il vous plaît (The bill, please)
- Je ne comprends pas (I don't understand)
- Pouvez-vous répéter ? (Can you repeat that?)
- Avez-vous des recommandations ? (Do you have any recommendations?)
- Quelle est la spécialité locale ? (What is the local specialty?)
- J'aimerais commander... (I would like to order...)
- Où se trouve la gare ? (Where is the train station?)
- Où sont les toilettes ? (Where are the toilets?)
- Pouvez-vous prendre une photo de moi ? (Can you take a picture of me?)

- Quel est le meilleur moyen de se déplacer en ville ? (What is the best way to get around the city?)
- Quand ouvre/ferme cet endroit ? (When does this place open/close?)
- Puis-je avoir un plan de la ville ? (Can I have a map of the city?)
- C'est délicieux ! (It's delicious!)
- Pouvez-vous me recommander un bon restaurant ? (Can you recommend a good restaurant?)
- Quelle est la météo aujourd'hui ? (What is the weather like today?)
- Je voudrais acheter des souvenirs. (I would like to buy some souvenirs.)
- Y a-t-il un marché près d'ici ? (Is there a market nearby?)
- J'ai une réservation au nom de... (I have a reservation under the name...)
- Où puis-je trouver un distributeur automatique ? (Where can I find an ATM?)
- Est-ce que je peux payer par carte de crédit ? (Can I pay by credit card?)
- Pouvez-vous me donner l'heure, s'il vous plaît ? (Can you tell me the time, please?)
- Quels sont les horaires d'ouverture ? (What are the opening hours?)
- Je suis perdu(e). (I am lost.)
- Est-ce loin d'ici ? (Is it far from here?)

- Quel est le numéro d'urgence ? (What is the emergency number?)
- J'aimerais réserver une chambre pour ce soir. (I would like to book a room for tonight.)
- Où puis-je prendre un taxi ? (Where can I find a taxi?)
- C'est magnifique ! (It's beautiful!)
- Comment puis-je aller à... ? (How can I get to...?)
- Puis-je avoir l'addition, s'il vous plaît ? (Can I have the bill, please?)
- C'est très gentil de votre part. (That's very kind of you.)
- Pouvez-vous me recommander un endroit calme pour se détendre ? (Can you recommend a quiet place to relax?)
- J'ai une allergie à... (I am allergic to...)
- Pouvez-vous m'indiquer un bon itinéraire touristique ? (Can you suggest a good tourist route?)
- C'est une expérience unique ! (It's a unique experience!)
- Quand part le prochain train/bus pour... ? (When does the next train/bus to... depart?)
- Pouvez-vous me donner un conseil de sécurité ? (Can you give me a safety tip?)
- Je voudrais essayer la spécialité locale. (I would like to try the local specialty.)
- Merci pour votre aide ! (Thank you for your help!)

Slang terms
- Chouette: Cool
- Bouquin: Book
- Truc: Thing
- Taf: Job
- Bagnole: Car
- Bof: Meh
- Pote: Friend
- Baraque: House
- Fringues: Clothes
- Bled: Small town
- Péter un plomb: Lose one's temper
- Kiffer: To enjoy
- Blé: Money
- Beuverie: Drinking spree
- Gosses: Kids
- Se planter: To make a mistake
- Zapper: To forget
- Piquer: To steal
- Zou: Let's go
- Flingue: Gun
- Choper: To catch
- Crèmerie: Ice cream shop
- Bosser: To work
- Se marrer: To laugh
- Plouc: Hick
- Kif-kif: Same
- Tchatcher: To chat

- Galère: Trouble
- Bousculer: To push around
- Flouze: Cash

Chapter 3

Hotels

Below are recommended hotels to take note of; Consider booking your hotel in advance; Online travel websites like Trivago.com and Booking.com can assist.

1. Hôtel Mercure Annecy Centre - Address: 26 Rue Vaugelas - Telephone: +33 4 50 45 59 80 - Description: Contemporary hotel in the heart of Annecy with cheerful rooms, free Wi-Fi, and a relaxed atmosphere.

2. ibis Annecy Centre Vieille Ville - Address: 12 Rue de la Gare, Ilôt De La Manufacture, Telephone: +33 4 50 45 43 21

Riverside getaway with contemporary accommodations, a bar and lounge open around-the-clock and free WiFi.

3. Annecy Hôtel du Nord, 24 Rue Sommeiller; tel. +33 4 50 45 08 78
Simple sanctuary in Annecy with uncomplicated rooms, complimentary Wi-Fi, and satellite TV for a relaxing stay.

4. Hotel Campanile Annecy Centre Gare, 37 Rue Vaugelas, +33 4 50 45 05 78
Modern housing with flat-screen TVs, free Wi-Fi, and a terrace, providing a straightforward yet stylish refuge.

5. Hôtel des Alpes
12 Rue de la Poste; contact number: +33 4 50 45 04 56
A chic retreat with vibrant rooms, free Wi-Fi, and a charming dining room that creates a relaxing atmosphere.

6. Hôtel Le Pélican - Address: 20 Rue des Marquisats - Telephone: +33 4 50 09 38 00 - Information: Elegant lakefront hotel with warmly furnished rooms, suites, and a sophisticated restaurant with tranquil lake views.

7. Atipik Hotel Annecy, 19 Rue Vaugelas; tel. +33 4 50 52 84 33

Warm, uniquely designed rooms with complimentary Wi-Fi, a bar and a delicious breakfast buffet choice for individualised comfort.

8. Hôtel du Château - Phone: +33 4 50 45 27 66 - Address: 16 Rpe du Château

- Description: Relaxed refuge in a historic stone building with a patio, guest lounge and Wi-Fi.

9. Les Trésoms Lake and Spa Resort, 15 Bd de la Corniche, contact information: +33 4 50 51 43 84

Elegant hotel from the 1930s with lake views, a café, a spa, an outdoor pool, and tennis for an opulent getaway.

10. Splendid Hotel, 4 Quai Eustache Chappuis; tel. +33 4 50 45 20 00

An informal hotel by a lake that offers free high-speed Internet, lake views, and a lounge with a terrace for a relaxing getaway.

11. Best Western Hôtel International, located at 5 Avenue du Thiou, may be reached at +334 502-353

The upscale refuge offers simple rooms, a restaurant, a cocktail lounge, and a spa for a lavish stay in Annecy.

12. Icone Hôtel - Annecy - Address: 1 Fbg des Balmettes - Telephone: +33 4 50 45 04 12 - Highlights: Quiet rooms with minibars, free WiFi, and a modern dining area in a simple, contemporary environment.

13. Hôtel des Marquisats, 6 Chem. de Colmyr; tel. +33 4 50 51 52 34
Flat-screen televisions, a sauna, a lounge/bar, a hammam and free parking are all features of these comfortable, rustic lodgings.

14. Best Western Plus Hôtel Carlton, located at 5 Rue des Glières, may be reached at + 334 50109009.
- Description: A practical budget hotel with free Wi-Fi and a chic bar that combines affordability and comfort.

15. Hotel du Palais de l'Isle Annecy, 13 Rue Perrière, +33 4 50 45 86 87
Low-key rooms with canal views are available in this 18th-century building, which also features a lounge and free WiFi.

Chapter 4

Restaurants

Try any of the best restaurants for a relaxed and enjoyable time below, along with their contact details.

escargot

- Chez Mamie Lise - Address: 11 Rue Grenette - Telephone: +33 4 50 45 41 18 - Description: Savoyard fondue and sweeping mountain views are offered at this rustic French Alpine restaurant.

- Le Rhône Bistro

  13 Avenue du Rhône, Paris, France +33 4 50 45 53 34

Refined stop for outstanding Rhône wine pairings and seasonal Alpine fare like tartiflette.

- Auberge de Savoie. Contact information: +33 4 50 45 03 05; Address: 1 Pl. Saint-François de Sales.

Elevated regional cuisine in chic surroundings, including classic raclette and delightful Savoyard ambience.

- L'Esquisse - Phone: +33 4 50 44 80 59 - Address: 21 Rue Royale

Elegant bistro serving delectable crozets and inventive French cuisine, famed for its Alpine cuisine.

- La Guinguette du 1er Mets, 2 Rue Saint-Maurice; +33 4 57 09 10 54

Escargot and handcrafted French tapas are available at this laid-back restaurant, which also serves unique seasonal dishes.

- Le Bouillon, 9 Rue de la Gare, phone: +33 4 50 77 31 02, is number six.

Seasonal food in relaxed surroundings, with boeuf bourguignon and a warm railway station ambiance.

- L'Etage, 13 Rue du Pâquier; tel. : +33 4 50 51 03 28

Relaxed establishment with great panoramic views and Alpine delicacies like tart au Beaufort.

- Le Denti, 25 Av. de Loverchy, phone: +33 4 50 64 21 17, address

Unassuming gourmet restaurant featuring escargot de Bourgogne and other diverse French specialties.

- Au Fil Du Thiou - Place des Cordeliers, 5 Pass. des Bains - Phone: +33 4 50 05 42 81 - Description: Casual restaurant serving inventive local dishes, including bouillabaisse and a canal-side dining atmosphere.

- Le Vertumne. Contact information: +33 4 50 45 92 96; Address: 13 Rue Sommeiller.

Seasonal cuisine in a cheerful setting with views of the bustling streets of Annecy and coq au vin.

- Le Pas Sage - Address: 6 Rue Joseph Blanc - Phone: +33 4 50 45 43 75 - Information: Casual eatery serving quiche Lorraine and leisurely French dining. Seasonal menu.

- COZNA - Phone: +33 4 50 65 00 25 - Address: 22 Fbg Sainte-Claire

Duck confit is one of the restaurant's inventive local dishes, and it has a quaint, romantic ambiance.

- BON PAIN BON VIN

Address: 17 Rue Filaterie; telephone number: +33 4 50 45 25 62

French bakery serving baguettes, croissants, and a delicious selection of pastries.

- Le Bilboquet - Address: 14 Fbg Sainte-Claire - Phone: +33 4 50 45 21 68 - Information: French food served in a lovely setting, including coq au vin.

- Le Chalet - Phone: +33 4 50 51 82 55 - Address: Quai de l'Évêché - Description: Cosy location for Alpine delicacies, offering raclette and cosy chalet-style environment.

- "Le Vieil Annecy" Restaurant, 13 Rue Perrière, Phone: +33 4 50 45 32 41

Relaxed restaurant featuring regional specialties, like escargot and traditional French comfort food.

Chapter 5

Attractions

Below are some of the Attractions in the city, both the popular and the less-known attractions with their addresses. Visit some or all of them, depending on the available time.

- Annecy's Musée-Château
- Address: Place du Château - Summary: Explore contemporary art exhibits within the alluring walls of a historic castle.

- Jardins de l'Europe - Address: Quai Napoléon III -Take in the grandeur of this lakeside park with views of the mountains, ideal for a leisurely stroll.

- Pont des Amours - Travel across the lovely Pont des Amours bridge while immersed in the lively atmosphere of Annecy.

- Cathédrale Saint-Pierre: Rue Jean-Jacques Rousseau

Discover the church and former monastery from the 16th century, a reminder of Annecy's lengthy past.

- Faubourg des Annonciades - Location: Fbg des Annonciades - Description: Explore the attraction that is Faubourg des Annonciades to experience its attractiveness.

- Basilique de la Visitation - Address: 11 Avenue de la Visitation - Information: Visit this church from the early 1900s for a unique view of Annecy.

- Ascension du Mont Blanc - Address: 1 Rue du Mont Blanc - Information: Discover the charm of this attraction, which has a unique personality.

- Water Fill Station - Address: 50 Rue Carnot - Information: Stop at the Water Fill Station to learn about the practical side of Annecy.

- Quai de l'Île - Location: Quai de l'Île - Description: Discover Quai de l'Île's splendour, an addition to Annecy's gorgeous shoreline.

- Le Pâquier - Address: Av. d'Albigny - Description: At Le Pâquier, take a leisurely stroll while surrounded by nature, wide-open spaces, and a picturesque lake.

- Parc Animalier de la Grande Jeanne - Address: 14 Rte du Semnoz - Description: Meet native species in this little animal park, which provides a distinctive experience for nature lovers.

- Côte Perrière - Location: 1 Côte Perrière - Explore Côte Perrière's appeal as a tourist destination with a unique charm.

- Place Notre-Dame.
  Discover Porte Notre-Dame's historical significance to give your trip to Annecy a historical flavour.

Chapter 6

Shopping

Below are some of the best types of shops in the city.

Try shopping in any of them and bring back some souvenirs home;

- Centre Commercial Carrefour Annecy, a shopping centre located at 134 Avenue de Genève in Annecy, France.

- Centre commercial Courier, a type of mall, is located at 65 Rue Carnot and can be reached at +33 4 50 46 46 76.

- Nouvelles Galeries Annecy - Address: 2BIS Rue Thomas Ruphy - Type: Shopping Mall

- Galeries Lafayette Annecy. This department store is located at 25 Av. du Parmelan and may be reached at +334 503-382-112.

- Galerie Commerçante - Address: 129 Av. de Genève, Type: Shopping Mall

- La Galerie Val Semnoz, a shopping centre located at 20 Av. de Périaz with phone number +33 4 50 10 97 96.

- Alpine Side, a sportswear retailer with a location at Centre Commercial Courier, 1 Pass Monge and a phone number at +33 4 50 67 35 76.

- CrushON - Galeries Lafayette Annecy - 25 Av. du Parmelan - Category: Vintage Clothing Store

- Maje Annecy - Category: Women's Clothing Shop - Location: 37 Rue Carnot - Contact Information: +33 4 50 51 77 92

- Les Palettes
Address: Galerie commerciale de l'Evéché, 9 Rue Royale, Type: Clothing Store, Phone: +33 4 50 27 77 17,

- Fashion Store
8 Quai de l'évêché 74000 Annecy- Clothing Store - Address: 8 Quai de l'Évêché - Telephone: +33 9 53 48 66 54

- Annecy Concept Shop, a sporting goods retailer with a location at 1 Rue Président Favre and a phone number at +33 4 50 51 41 56.

- Grenet'Shop - Category: Pen Shop - Location: 2 Rue Saint-Maurice - Contact Information: +33 4 50 51 16 74

- Don't call me, Jennyfer is a youth clothing retailer store with an address at 65 Rue Carnot and phone number +33 4 50 46 84 89.

Chapter 7

Leisure Activities

Below are more activities and Excursions to be involved in the city;

- Experience the thrill of paragliding with Delta Escape's vivacious and qualified team while flying above Lake Annecy.

- Between €85 and €150.

- Location: 14.9 kilometres from Annecy. Fly over the stunning Lake Annecy, where each glide awakens a fantasy. Your safety is ensured by qualified pilots, making it an exciting experience for all skill levels.

- An exhilarating canyoning descent to Lake Annecy Beginner/Intermediate Level: Take a 3 or 5-hour descent in the Canyon d'Angon near Lake Annecy to experience the thrill of canyoning.

- Price: €55.

Location: 11.3 kilometres from Annecy. Discover Lake Annecy's breathtaking south shore, where the Canyon d'Angon provides exhilarating thrills. It's an unforgettable journey led by knowledgeable guides.

- Canoeing along the Cheran River - Take your family on a canoeing excursion in the Bauges mountains close to Annecy.

- Price: €69.
- Distance: 12.2 kilometres from Annecy.
- Navigate the Chéran river as it is snow melting, a thrilling and one-of-a-kind adventure. There are numerous routes available, guaranteeing a day full of enjoyment for everyone.

- First Paraglider Flight in Annecy - Fly in a paraglider for the first time with K2, a 2005-founded school that places an emphasis on safety and flying.

- Price range: €85–€190.
- Address: Doussard.

- The founders, Maxence and Christophe, establish a setting where safety and the exhilaration of flight coexist. K2 guarantees a kind and unforgettable experience, regardless of whether you're a novice or looking for more challenging courses.

Chapter 8

Festivals and events
Attending some of the events listed below in the city or nearby can help make your travelling memorable.

- The Annecy International Animated Film Festival, which is held in France's Annecy.
- June, 2024

An international meeting of movie buffs and animators exhibiting the greatest in animated film.

- Annecy Venetian Carnival - Date: February 2024 - Location: Annecy, France - Description: Dive into the mystique and beauty of the Venetian carnival, celebrated with grandeur and elegance.

- Musilac - Date: July 2024 - Location: Aix-les-Bains, France - Description: Musilac is the finest music festival in Savoy set against the picturesque setting of Aix-les-Bains.

- Idéklic - Moirans-en-Montagne, France - Date: July 2024 - Description: A colourful worldwide festival that encourages innovation and delight for young performers, viewers, and creators.

- Evian Championship - Location: Évian-les-Bains, France - Date: September 2023 - Watch the top female golfers compete at the famous Evian Championship, one of France's premier golf competitions.

- Grande Odyssée Savoie Mont Blanc

Locations: Les Carroz-d'Arâches, Les Gets, Praz de Lys-Sommand, Megève, Pralognan-la-Vanoise, La

Plagne, Val-Cenis, Aussois, Bessans, and La Léchère.

One of the largest international dog sledge races ever will take place in beautiful locales in January 2024.

- Alps Bike Festival - La Clusaz, France - Date: June 2024 - During the thrilling Alps Bike Festival, go on a mountain riding trip in the picturesque Aravis mountains.

- New Beaujolais Festival - Dates: November 16–19, 2023 – Description: Celebrate the customary release of new Beaujolais wine, a beloved cultural occasion held all over the country.

- European Museum Night - Date: May 2024 - Information: Enjoy a fun-filled and educational evening of exploration in museums all over France on this special occasion.

- Rendez-vous aux Jardins Garden event - Date: June 2024 - Description: The event honours the beauty of gardens around France and serves as a gathering place for people who enjoy nature and plants.

- On June 21, 2024, join the nation-wide celebration of music diversity for World Music Day, which will feature a variety of musical genres for all audiences.

- Tour de France - Date: July 2024 - Take in the historic Tour de France, a legendary cycling event that personifies top-tier riding.

- French National Day - Date: July 14, 2024 - Description: Mark French National Day with symbolic celebrations honouring the demise of absolute monarchy and national unity.

- European Heritage Days - Date: September 2023 - Information: Discover France's rich cultural heritage at this autumn's enthralling European Heritage Days, an event that reveals the nation's varied history.

- French Cuisine Festival, which will take place from November 16 to November 19, 2023.

Enjoy the French Cuisine Festival, a lovely display of the country's culinary treasures, as it honours the culinary legacy of France.

Chapter 9

Itinerary

Below is a detailed 6 days Itinerary suggestions, you can adjust your based on your preference and timing.

Day 1: Gastronomic Delights
- In the morning, take a stroll down Av. d'Albigny while taking in the tranquil Le Pâquier.
- For lunch, visit the chic L'Esquisse at 21 Rue Royale to savour Alpine cuisine.
- In the afternoon, take in Annecy's attractiveness and make sure to visit Plage des Marquisats, a grassy lakefront beach.
- For dinner, enjoy French Alpine cuisine on the patio at Les Chineurs de la Cuisine.

Day Two: Lakeside Views
- In the morning, visit the bustling Quai de l'Évêché Farmers Market in Annecy.
- In the afternoon, unwind at the Gare d'Annecy and take in the distinctive ambiance of the train station.
- At dusk, explore the area around the station looking for undiscovered attractions.

Day 3: Architecture and History

- Morning: Commence your tour of Annecy's historic beauty at Gare d'Annecy.
- Lunch: For a quick meal, pick a neighbourhood café or boulangerie.
- In the afternoon, stroll down Rue Sainte-Claire and take in the artwork of Les Chineurs de la Cuisine.
- In the evening, take in Annecy's glowing splendour.

A cultural experience on day four
- In the morning, start your day at Le Pâquier and appreciate its cultural significance.
- Lunch: Visit L'Esquisse on Rue Royale for a delectable meal.
Visit the Gare d'Annecy in the afternoon while appreciating its historical significance.
- For dinner, visit any lakeside restaurant to indulge in regional cuisine.

Day 5: Retreat to a lake
- Morning: Enjoy a peaceful morning at Plage des Marquisats to start your day.
- Lunch: For a lovely meal, pick a café along a lake.
- In the afternoon, go along Av. d'Albigny and take in the scenery beside the lake.
- Dinner: Enjoy another evening of delectable Alpine cuisine at L'Esquisse.

Day six: The market day Morning: Enter the bustling ambiance of the Quai de l'Évêché Farmers Market in Annecy.

- Afternoon: Take it easy and explore Gare d'Annecy's distinctive transit culture.

- In the evening, say goodbye to your travel companions over dinner at Les Chineurs de la Cuisine as you reflect on the charm of Annecy and the flavours of the Alps.

Self-Reflection questions

Below are some personal questions, answering them can help enrich your travel experience. Safe trip

Travel reflection can strengthen your relationship with the places you go, promote personal development, and increase the significance of your experiences. Self-reflection questions let you analyse your feelings and thoughts, giving you insightful information that goes beyond simple sightseeing. To get ready for a life-changing experience, think about these questions before starting your trip to Annecy.

Prior to departure:
1. What expectations do you have as you prepare to travel to Annecy, and how can they affect how you view the city?

_____

_____

_____

_____

_____

_____

_____

2. What parts of Annecy's history, culture, or cuisine most pique your interest, and how do you think knowing about them can improve your trip?

_____

_____

_____

_____

_____

_____

_____

_____

3. Consider your previous trip experiences. Are there any good habits or behaviours you wish to continue from past travels, as well as any obstacles you want to overcome in Annecy?

_____

_____

_____

_____

_____

_____

_____

4. Take into account the kind of tourist you wish to be in Annecy. What actions will you take to be a considerate tourist and how will you interact with the local community?

_____
_____
_____
_____
_____
_____
_____
_____

5. Visualise the perfect ratio of organised activity to unplanned exploration. How will you make room in your schedule for unforeseen connections and discoveries?

_____
_____
_____
_____
_____
_____
_____
_____

After your journey:
1. Having explored Annecy, how did the actual experience correspond to your expectations, and how did it alter or challenge your preconceived notions?

_____

_____

_____

_____

_____

_____

_____

_____

2. Consider specific events or encounters during your time in Annecy that left a lasting impression on you. How have these encounters affected your worldview or core principles?

_____

_____

_____

_____

_____

_____

_____

3. Take into account any cultural nuances you encountered. What understandings about the interconnection of cultures did you obtain by navigating and appreciating these differences?

_____

_____

_____

_____

_____

_____

_____

_____

4. Consider the difficulties you encountered while travelling. What obstacles did you face, how did you overcome them, and what abilities or strengths did you uncover about yourself?

_____

_____

_____

_____

_____

_____

_____

5. As you head back home, consider what you miss most about Annecy. How can you incorporate these fresh inspirations or admirations into your routine to keep feeling connected and growing?

_____

_____

_____

_____

Note:

Note:

Printed in Great Britain
by Amazon

43072845R00030